Lance's Dragon

A Division of The McGraw-Hill Companies

Columbus, Ohio

www.sra4kids.com

SRA/McGraw-Hill

*A Division of The **McGraw·Hill** Companies*

Send all inquiries to:
SRA/McGraw-Hill
8787 Orion Place
Columbus, OH 43240-4027

ISBN 0-07-569501-4
    3 4 5 6 7 8 9 DBH 05 04 03 02

"Wake up!" yelled Lance's mom.
"Cedric the Dragon has taken my
bracelet and scarf!"

Lance was brave.
"Cedric is a bad dragon," he said.
Lance raced out after Cedric.

Lance walked into a cave. He saw Cedric and
saw hot flames by Cedric's face.
"I do not like this place," said Lance.

But Lance was brave.
He grabbed the lace scarf, and
flames licked his face.

Then Cedric felt bad.
"I will give back the scarf and the bracelet,"
Cedric said.

Cedric helped Lance and his mom bake apple
tarts and bread.
Cedric ate a tart and stopped being bad.